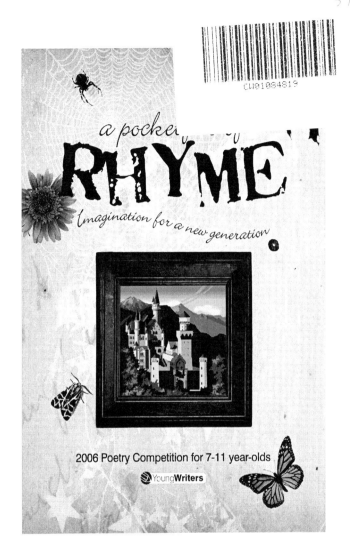

a pocket

RHYME

Imagination for a new generation

2006 Poetry Competition for 7-11 year-olds

YoungWriters

Poems From Central England

Edited by Donna Samworth

 Young**Writers**

First published in Great Britain in 2007 by:
Young Writers
Remus House
Coltsfoot Drive
Peterborough
PE2 9JX
Telephone: 01733 890066
Website: www.youngwriters.co.uk

SB ISBN 1 84602 715 2

Foreword

Young Writers was established in 1991 and has been passionately devoted to the promotion of reading and writing in children and young adults ever since. The quest continues today. Young Writers remains as committed to the nurturing of poetic and literary talent as ever.

This year's Young Writers competition has proven as vibrant and dynamic as ever and we are delighted to present a showcase of the best poetry from across the UK and in some cases overseas. Each poem has been selected from a wealth of *A Pocketful Of Rhyme* entries before ultimately being published in this, our fourteenth primary school poetry series.

Once again, we have been supremely impressed by the overall quality of the entries we have received. The imagination, energy and creativity which has gone into each young writer's entry made choosing the poems a challenging and often difficult but ultimately hugely rewarding task - the general high standard of the work submitted ensured this opportunity to bring their poetry to a larger appreciative audience.

We sincerely hope you are pleased with this final collection and that you will enjoy *A Pocketful Of Rhyme Poems From Central England* for many years to come.

Contents

Tom Dearing (10)	38
Liam McCullion (10)	39
Daniel Jefferson (10)	40
Josh Hamilton (11)	41
Cheryl Selby (10)	42
Ellie-Mae Shepherd (10)	43
Bradley McKenzie (11)	44
Abigail Smith (10)	45
Laura Houldridge (11)	46
Olivia Peace (10)	47
Kieran Binns (11)	48
Melissa Stabler (10)	49
Emily Benstead Sale (10)	50
Holly Waites (8)	51

Dosthill School, Tamworth

Georgia Tuckey (7)	52

Great Dalby Primary School, Melton Mowbray

Amber Allen (9)	53
Tommy Smith (8)	54
Alisha Brown (9)	55
Rowena Burke (8)	56
Verity Topham (8)	57
Emily Booth (9)	58
Abi Lucia Brown (9)	59
Alex Murray (9)	60
Alex Kirk (8)	61
Emma Sunderland (9)	62
Luke Johnson (9)	63
Thomas Kowalski (9)	64
Luke Harrison (10)	65
Bethany Houghton (9)	66
Niamh Gibson (10)	67
Lydia Hall (9)	68
Georgia Boorn (9)	69
Harry Wells (10)	70
Dan Turner (8)	71
Sophie Lee (10)	72
Mollie Brooks (10)	73
Harry Jinks (11)	74

Matt Kuzmicz (10)	75
Leah Topham (10)	76
Rebecca Bond (10)	77
Charlotte Brown (10)	78
Toby Heaver (10)	79
Lucy Sparling (10)	80
Edward Groom (10)	81
Rosie Burrows (10)	82
Hannah Burrows (10)	83
Adam Wright (10)	84
Hetty Burke (10)	85
Georgina Kilpatrick (10)	86
Megan Story (10)	87

Highley Primary School, Highley

Selina Jones (9)	88
Tim Resch (10)	89
Will Bloomer (10)	90
David Hartmann (9)	91
Rebecca Phillips (9)	92
Joshua Ward (10)	93
Jack Broome (10)	94
Ben Richards (10)	95
Danielle Walker (10)	96
Gregory Stevens (9)	97
Ellie Jones (9)	98

Lees Primary School, Keighley

Joseph Wilmore (10)	99
Jethro Rainford (10)	100
Liam Walsh (10)	101
Samuel Treece (10)	102
Charlotte Brown (10)	103
Benjamin Dixon (10)	104
Jack Kavanagh (10)	105
Bethany Nixon (10)	106
Hannah Inman (10)	107
Connor Fox (10)	108
Adele Cowan (10)	109
Jodie Packer (10)	110
Natalie Stephens (10)	111

Victoria Milner (10)   112
Courtney Dunstan (10)   113
Rebecca Williams (10)   114
Alex Simkins (10)   115
Rhys Hart (10)   116
Taylor Robinson (11)   117
Ellie Thornton (10)   118
Lauren Pedley (10)   119
Adrian Wilson (10)   120

Northfield Road Primary School, Dudley
Emily Smout (9)   121
Darrin Tucker (9)   122
Bethany Sidaway (9)   123
Karine Gilbert (9)   124
Amber-Leigh Evans (10)   125
Tina Sultana (9)   126
Alice Cox (9)   127
Hajra Begum (9)   128
Elizabeth Willetts (9)   129
Bethany Wood (9)   130
Kerry Burgoyne (9)   131
Abidah Sultana (9)   132
Mathew Rogers (9)   133
Keiran Parkes (9)   134
Nicola Handley (9)   135
Amina Bibi (9)   136
Natasha Bird (9)   137
Ellie Cove (9)   138
Bibi Muriyam (9)   139
Sulaiman Janjua (9)   140
James Whittingham (9)   141
Liam Whitcombe (9)   142
Caleb Burchell (9)   143
Bradley Hanson (9)   144
Christopher Hodgetts (9)   145
Liam Haycock (9)   146

Offmore First School, Kidderminster
Adam Dalton (8)   147
Owen Scott (8)   148

The Poems

Elephant

Ear flapper
Tree mover
Food sucker
Loud trumper
Stampede maker
Circus entertainer
Slow traveller
Massive mammal
Water blaster
Disney star.

Ellie Chan (10)

Sunshine

The sun is vast
The sun is hot,
Like a great big pot.

The sun is boiling
The sun gets hotter
Like a large engine!

The sun is the best
The sun is good for ice cream weather,
Yum-yum!

The sun is excellent for people on the beach,
The sun is the greatest!
Everyone knows!

Tom Young (8)
Cavendish Primary School, Hull

The Wind

The wind can be warm
The wind can be cold
The wind can be strong
Like a person big and bold

The wind can be hurricane
Swirling all around
The wind can pull you over
And make a quiet sound.

Jack Kearney (9)
Cavendish Primary School, Hull

The Wild Wind

The wind can be rough
The wind can be tough
The wind can be calm
Like a lake in spring

The wind can be nice
The wind can be annoying
The wind can be mad
Like a dog chasing a cat.

Lauren Jackson (8)
Cavendish Primary School, Hull

Hailstones

Hailstones can be huge
Hailstones can be tiny
Like an ant

Hailstones can be as thick
As a piece of card
Hailstones can be white as milk
Like a polar bear.

Michael Rowley (8)
Cavendish Primary School, Hull

Wind On The Way

Stormy winds are on the way
Hurricanes are on the way
Tornadoes are on the way
Cold weather is on the way
Gales are on the way
Trouble is on the way.

Alex Rickles (8)
Cavendish Primary School, Hull

The Wind

The wind can twist
The wind can turn
The wind can dodge
Like a rugby player in a match.

The wind can spin
The wind can dance
The wind can gust
Like a cat and mouse playing.

The wind can be fierce
The wind can be calm
The wind can be strong
Like a wrestler fighting.

The wind can be quiet
The wind can be calm
The wind can be sleepy
Like a sleeping cat snoozing.

Victoria Peace (8)
Cavendish Primary School, Hull

The Wind

The wind can be rough
The wind can be tough
The wind can be mad
Like a football player swerving

The wind can be gentle
The wind can be angry
The wind can be nice.

Daniel Shepherd (9)
Cavendish Primary School, Hull

Hailstone

Hailstones can be big
Hailstones can be small
Hailstones can be rough
Hailstones can be tough
Hailstones can be as white as a cloud.

Mason Varney (8)
Cavendish Primary School, Hull

The Wonderful Wind

The wind is a wonderful thing,
It blows to the left and then to the right,
Just like a dog's tail,
As the dog's trying to catch it with a *bite!*

As it swoops - and sweeps to another place
Flying past a child's face,
While the tail does its strange dance,
With a trance and a prance,
Though the wind is still a wonderful thing.

Lauren Sanderson (9)
Cavendish Primary School, Hull

The Wind

The wind can be calm.
A cool, gentle feeling
Whistling through your fingers
It glides round people far and near,
Like a fish swimming softly in the sea.
But, if the wind gets cross . . .
It will turn into a hurricane
Sucking up earth!
Whirling and twirling angrily,
Like a bully taking over the world.

Sophie Jameson (8)
Cavendish Primary School, Hull

The Sun

The sun can be calm,
The sun can be hot,
The sun can be bursting bright,
The sun can be nice and warm,

The sun can be boiling.
The sun can glow
The sun can be kind and friendly,
The sun can be glamorous,
The sun is like an enormous fireball.

Sophie Raven (9)
Cavendish Primary School, Hull

The Foggy Air

The cloudy air above the ground.
It's misty and blurry.
It charges at me like a hound.
It looks furry.

Adam Waudby (8)
Cavendish Primary School, Hull

The Blizzard

The blizzard is wild
The blizzard is powerful
The blizzard is angry
Like a raging sea

The blizzard is windy
The blizzard is snowy
The blizzard is hard
Like a person throwing water bombs.

Millica Morris (9)
Cavendish Primary School, Hull

The Sun

The sun can be hot
The sun can't be cold
The sun is a fireball red and bold.
The sun can be strong
The sun can be tough
The sun can be a fire truck
Bright and red.

Noah Jones (8)
Cavendish Primary School, Hull

The Sun

The sun is hot like a big boulder.
The sun is like a burning wave.
The sun is a big yellow page.

The sun is a burning friend
Every night and day.

Mark Shimmin (8)
Cavendish Primary School, Hull

The Wind

The wind can blow
The wind can howl
Like a wolf at night

The wind can be angry
The wind can be tough
The wind can be powerful
Like a wrestling bear.

Danny Symes (8)
Cavendish Primary School, Hull

Cold Days

Cold days make you icy
Cold days make you shiver
Cold days make you frozen
Cold days make you take a bath.

Ben Matos-Gois (8)
Cavendish Primary School, Hull

The Wind

The wind can be calm
The wind can be flat
The wind can be gentle
Like a dog on a mat

It can roar
It can blow a gale
It can snap
A gigantic nail

The wind can be warm
The wind can be strong
It can make the
Church bell go ding-dong.

Ben McKenzie (8)
Cavendish Primary School, Hull

The Sun

The sun can be boiling
The sun can be scorching
The sun can be like a fiery-red bird
The sun can clear a black rainy sky
The sun can be tough
The sun can be like a fiery boulder.

Matthew Todd (8)
Cavendish Primary School, Hull

Windy Days

Windy days can be cold.
Windy days can be freezing.
Windy days can make you freeze.
Windy days can make the trees rustle.
Windy days can blow the bushes.
The wind is like a stallion jumping in the breeze.

Farrah Moulson (8)
Cavendish Primary School, Hull

The Wind

The wind can be calm
The wind can be rough
The wind can also be very tough
It blows left and right like an angry fish.

The wind can be soft
The wind can be cool
The wind can also be a right fool
Blowing all the leaves off the trees
And sometimes it gets that angry it turns into a hurricane.

Molly Morrow (8)
Cavendish Primary School, Hull

The Snow

The snow can melt on your wellies
It crackles as you step on it.
You can step on the snow like a giant in a town
Or a bulldozer smashing down a city.

Alex Binns (8)
Cavendish Primary School, Hull

The Sun

The sun can be scorching,
The sun can be burning hot,
The sun can be boiling,
Like a giant fireball.

The sun is enormous and gigantic,
The sun is calm,
The sun is nice and warm,
Like a long fur rug.

Casey Vee Johnson (8)
Cavendish Primary School, Hull

The Wind

The wind can be quiet
The wind can be loud
The wind can be rough
The wind can be tough
The wind can be a breeze
The wind can be wild
The wind can dance
The wind can act like a cat
It's like a sleeping cat.

Caitlin Smith (8)
Cavendish Primary School, Hull

The Wind

The wind can be loud,
The wind can be soft,
The wind can be calm,
The wind can be quiet.

The wind can be tough,
The wind can be hard,
The wind can be rough,
The wind can be like a bully in a rage.

Chloe Nicholson (8)
Cavendish Primary School, Hull

The Wind

The wind can be flat
The wind can be calm
The wind can be gentle
Like a snoozing cat.

It can roar
It can blow a gale
It can knock over
A boat's sail.

The wind can be warm
The wind can be cold
Young kids will say
It is boiling.

Christopher Mee (8)
Cavendish Primary School, Hull

The Sun

The sun can be hot
The sun can be bright
The sun is like a football player's strike

The sun can be warm
The sun can be boiling
The sun burns you
Like a roasting chicken on a stove.

The sun can make you sweaty
The sun can blaze like a glowing fire.

Thomas Michael Quest **(8)**
Cavendish Primary School, Hull

The Wind

The wind can be calm,
Like a sleeping cat,
The wind can be strong
And blow away the flowers.

The wind has muscles
It's very strong,
The wind's like a galloping horse,
It's going far and wide.

Chloe Parker (8)
Cavendish Primary School, Hull

The Orange Ocean

The sun shines brightly,
On the ocean floor,
I look out at sea,
As though through a door.

I feel the waves on the shore,
As I look at the blue sky,
Look at the orange ocean,
Because soon you'll say goodbye.

The sand is soft
The waves are calm,
The birds are high,
Now it is time.

The sun shines brightly,
On the ocean floor,
I look out at sea,
As though through an ocean door.

Joseph Jordan (10)
Cavendish Primary School, Hull

Slithery Stream

In the secret land of peace,
There's something flowing like a dream,
It's shining in the dazzling sun,
It is the calm, slithery stream.

I sail along in my large boat,
There's no gale,
I see a yacht,
As big as a whale.

Rachel Naulls (10)
Cavendish Primary School, Hull

The Crashing Ocean

The hungry sea as black as night,
It comes to the shore dashing,
Like an Olympic sprinter going for gold,
But I like it when it comes crashing.

The clouds are as black as night,
And rain comes pouring down,
Hammering down on the rough sea,
The lightning is running the town.

No fish swim in the sea,
It is much too rough,
Some people swim in the sea,
But they have to be tough.

Lloyd Varney (10)
Cavendish Primary School, Hull

The Slithery Stream

The sun shines so brightly,
The water is trickling,
Slowly down the mountain,
Splishing, splashing, sploshing.

Water rushing into the rivers,
Slosh, a galoshing slosh, a galoshing,
Light bright, almost see-through waters,
And the water is so loudly crashing.

The water begins to get rough,
Boats are overturned very quickly,
Everyone ends up in the water,
Heading towards the waterfall,

The sun shines so brightly,
The water is trickling,
Slowly down the mountain,
Splishing, splashing, sploshing.

Cassie Riley (10)
Cavendish Primary School, Hull

The Slithering River

The slithering river is a long thin snake,
Eating away at the black pebbles.
The sun beams down and the sand needs a rake,
It is as rough as a lizard's skin.

The sun is hot and the river is calm,
The river is as blue as a dolphin in the sea.
The river is as smooth as a baby's palm,
And it is as warm as toasted toast.

The river is beautiful and very kind,
The windmills are going round very slow
You can dig all day long and treasure you will find
By the end of the day you will be really tired.

The slithering river is a long thin snake
Eating away at the black pebbles.
The sun beams down and the sand needs a rake,
It is as rough as a lizard's skin.

Eleanor Mead (10)
Cavendish Primary School, Hull

The Smashing Black Ocean

The creepy black ocean is crashing on the rocks,
Icy cold water has waves that crash,
Mountainous waves that smash and clash,
Black dirty ocean bang and bash.

Stormy and windy the thundering sky,
Cloudy, raining, making a splash,
The waves roll in with a dash,
Invading black clouds travelling by.

Unpleasant black sea surrounds us,
Dull is the growing grey sky,
Gloomy stars are passing by,
No silence on the land none at all.

The creepy black ocean is crashing on the rocks,
Icy cold water has waves that crash,
Mountainous waves that smash and clash,
Black dirty ocean bang and bash.

Tilly Taylor (10)
Cavendish Primary School, Hull

The Lashing Deep Blue

The sea is a writhing monster,
Lashing away at the beach,
Claiming all the stones and pebbles,
Into its cold, icy reach.

Breakers crashing out of the black,
Breaking on rock after rock,
This monster has only one fear,
The ever-changing clock.

The deep sea is violent,
Pushing further towards the land,
But retreating twice everyday
So people can enjoy the golden sand.

The sea is a writhing great monster,
Lashing away at the beach,
Claiming all the stones and pebbles,
Into its cold, icy reach.

Adam Cook (10)
Cavendish Primary School, Hull

The Terror Tide

Don't go near Terror Tide,
It'll suck you up like sand,
The waves go smashing through,
It sounds like a big *brass band!*

The black night creeps towards the rocks,
Yellow lightning lights the land
The lashing waves making a crash,
Grey and nasty grains of sand!

Flying through the ocean's waves
Something sharp and grey,
Lurking by the sandy shore,
Ready to betray.

Don't go near Terror Tide
It'll suck you up like sand,
The waves go smashing through
It sounds like a big *brass band.*

Emma Gale (10)
Cavendish Primary School, Hull

The Perfect Storm

The perfect storm is lashing
The thunderous waves are splashing
The water sprints up the beach
But luckily I'm out of reach

The wave grows up to an enormous height
As it roars back into the night
The people on land can't stand the fright
As they run back into the night.

Tom Dearing (10)
Cavendish Primary School, Hull

Obliterating Storm

The ocean's asleep
The ocean's deep
The ocean will roar
With its mighty claw
The waves are low
But soon they grow
20ft high
Up to the sky . . .

The thunder shall crash
The hail will bash
The rain shall spitter
The moon will glitter
The ocean is a mighty beast
Gulping sailors having a feast!

The ship will sink
The engine will clink
'We are doomed!'
The ship will go *boom!*
Time is ticking
My fingers are clicking.

The ocean's asleep
The ocean's deep
So the ocean can roar
With its mighty claw
We be no more
The waves are low
But soon they grow
20ft high.
Up to the sky . . .

Liam McCullion (10)
Cavendish Primary School, Hull

The Thrashing Ocean

The thrashing ocean is a fierce beast,
Washing up and down,
The waves are bashing against the rocks,
And the sea is a muddy-brown.

The weather is thrashing,
The rain pours down,
The thunder is hitting
Going round and round.

Daniel Jefferson (10)
Cavendish Primary School, Hull

The Crunching Ocean

The crunching ocean crunches away,
At the sandy beach all throughout the day,
The mountainous waves dash towards me,
Like a bee charging to sting me.

The lashing waves strike the rocks,
The thunder and lightning sparks the docks,
The monster in the darkness creeps up the beach,
Like a very speedy leech.

Josh Hamilton (11)
Cavendish Primary School, Hull

The Calm Turquoise Sea

The calm turquoise sea is a beautiful thing, washing up and down on the shores
There's swaying palm trees in the ocean breeze
Their beauty surrounds me
Rolling hills vast and green over the horizon I see.
Being at the sea is a wonderful thing, just you and me.

The weather at sea is always stunning
The sun beating down on the ground
The sea is as hot as a galaxy of burning stars.

Cheryl Selby (10)
Cavendish Primary School, Hull

The Crashing Waves

The crashing waves are like hungry wolves
Charging onto the beach
The pebbles are forever rolling in
But the islands are out of reach

Stormy and windy the black, black sky
The icy cold winds get louder
Flying over the colossal walls,
The birds look like white powder.

Ellie-Mae Shepherd (10)
Cavendish Primary School, Hull

The Raging Sea

The lethal sea is angry,
Lashing out at the golden beach,
The fish are frantically swimming,
Hoping to stay out of reach.

The clouds are as black as a bull,
The rain is hammering down on the sea,
Hitting the gigantic green waves,
Crashing down faster than a bee.

Fish swirling around in the current,
They're gradually losing control,
Night-time taking its advantage,
Little fish disappearing in a hole.

The lethal sea is angry,
Lashing out at the golden beach,
The fish are frantically swimming,
Hoping to stay out of reach.

Bradley McKenzie (11)
Cavendish Primary School, Hull

The Raging River

The raging river is a hungry cheetah,
Fast and very bold,
Mountainous waves in the fading sun,
So the river is icy cold.

The sky is a horrible black,
Just like a gigantic bull,
Lashing great river waves,
Which look very dull.

The raging river is freezing cold,
Its tides are sucking people in,
It's trying to get to me,
But luckily it's not going to win.

The raging river is a hungry cheetah,
Fast and very bold,
Mountainous waves in the fading sun,
So the river is icy cold.

Abigail Smith (10)
Cavendish Primary School, Hull

Lethal Ocean

The lethal ocean is hungry,
And it's coming at the beach
For more,
It's crushing hard waves on the
Rock sides,
But swishing on the soft ocean floor.

The hard winter blackness,
Beating at the sea,
I scurry away on the cliff sides,
But luckily I'm out of reach.

The icy sea is stronger,
And the waves are getting cold,
If you're swimming you will be swept away,
If you're young or old.

The lethal ocean is hungry,
And it's coming at the beach
For more,
It's crushing hard waves on the
Rock sides,
But swishing on the soft ocean floor.

Laura Houldridge (11)
Cavendish Primary School, Hull

The Crashing Ocean Waves

The fierce sea comes crashing down
The screaming winds break every gate
The ferocious sea comes lashing out,
As the ocean arrives very late.

The clouds look down over the sky,
The mountainous waves are wet,
The moon makes the oceans roar;
As the raging breakers storm the seas.

The sea is very stormy,
The pitch-black sea is not peach,
As the ocean takes the sand away,
Away from the lovely warm beach.

The rain starts to drip,
The sea is very watery,
The ocean roars, the ocean snores,
As the moon beats down from the sky.

Olivia Peace (10)
Cavendish Primary School, Hull

Mysterious Mountainside

The valleys, the caves and the caverns,
The gaps in the walls all hide,
The dense and dripping rivers,
Of the mysterious mountainside.

The sun beats down on the miniature lakes,
No clouds are in the skies,
The water trickles down the cracks,
Of the mysterious mountainside.

The small blue ponds rest on the top,
The reservoirs down the side,
The rain starts to drip on the rocky case,
Of the mysterious mountainside.

The storm overtakes the sky now,
No weather left is mild,
The lightning strikes the skyward trees,
Of the mysterious mountainside.

The valleys, the caves and the caverns,
The gaps in the walls all hide,
The dense and dripping rivers,
Of the mysterious mountainside.

Kieran Binns (11)
Cavendish Primary School, Hull

The Double-Faced Ocean

The double-faced ocean is a roaring fight,
Splashing away at the breakers,
Smashing and crashing into the night,
He is the mountainous wave makers

The sea can give you a lot of fright,
When you are there in the moonlight,
The sea attacks onto the sand,
If you are not careful it will catch you with its almighty hand.

The lightning will smash,
And the thunder will crash.
The time is now late,
To surrender your fate.

The double-faced ocean is a roaring fight,
Splashing away at the breakers,
Smashing and crashing into the night,
He is the mountainous wave makers.

Melissa Stabler (10)
Cavendish Primary School, Hull

The Lazy Waves

Water and waves are still sleeping,
Relaxing in the sun.
But still there is a quiet roaring,
As the day goes on.

Clear as blue-tinted glass,
But cold as melting ice.
Seaweed is like the sea's long grass,
Swishing in the ripples.

Fish diving in and out,
Playing as the day goes by.
Cod, goldfish and trout,
Diving in the sea.

The slightest ripple, a gentle flow,
Sparkling clear water,
With a twinkling glow,
Gently laps where sea meets sand.

Water and waves still sleeping,
Relaxing in the sun.
But still there is a quiet roaring,
As the day goes on.

Emily Benstead Sale (10)
Cavendish Primary School, Hull

The Wind

Wind is breeze
Move with ease
Rustles leaves.

Holly Waites (8)
Cavendish Primary School, Hull

Friends

Friends, friends and all of the rest
Forever and always
Yes, you are the best!
To walk through the hallways
To play with at lunch
To have a game of tig
Oops, what have you done?
There to help each other
To pick up off the floor
Friends, friends and all of the rest
Forever and always
Yes, you are the best!

Georgia Tuckey (7)
Dosthill School, Tamworth

The Doors Creep Open

The doors creep open
Nobody is there
But a tall dark shadow
Threatening to scare.

The dust blows up
With angry fear.
Skeletons whisper, 'I'll get you,'
Cold and clear.

Never come back
Or never go out
It's up to you
So you better
Watch out!

Amber Allen (9)
Great Dalby Primary School, Melton Mowbray

Sisters

Sisters are annoying
Sisters are a pain
Sometimes I just wish
I could shove mine down the drain

When my sister goes in my room
And I turn and chuck her out
She just turns and looks at me
And starts to scream and shout.

My sister is a selfish girl
I just wind her up
But all she does
Is get really fed up.

Tommy Smith (8)
Great Dalby Primary School, Melton Mowbray

Snowflakes

Snowflakes fall on my nose at Christmas
They make the garden gleam
When it is finished I'll go out and play
And go sledging all of the day!

You can make snowmen
With button-eyes and a carrot-nose
And a black hat and colourful nose
And a black hat and colourful scarf
It is so much fun!

Alisha Brown (9)
Great Dalby Primary School, Melton Mowbray

The Man In The Moon

The moon is like a big button
Shining all night
I wish it could come up to me
So I can take a big bite
When I stand in my porch
It looks like a big torch
As I lay in my bed
It shines on my head
I look up I see a face
It's the man in the moon!
I hear a whisper saying, 'I'll see you soon!'

Rowena Burke (8)
Great Dalby Primary School, Melton Mowbray

The Ginger Cat

My ginger cat likes playing with string
She sleeps in the sun
When she gets hot she goes inside
To get some cold milk she slurps from a bowl.

I take her to the park
I throw a ball of string
My cat runs after it
She brings it back
Then we go home to sleep.

Verity Topham (8)
Great Dalby Primary School, Melton Mowbray

The Polar Bear

The polar bear gallops over the crisp white snow,
Chasing her newborn cub
They wander around the seals
Who have their heads low
The seals look up and waddle away
Into the far, far north wind.

Emily Booth (9)
Great Dalby Primary School, Melton Mowbray

Thunder

When it starts to thunder
I know it's going to rain
I see the lightning strike
In the darkness of the sky
Boom, boom, boom goes the thunder
As the whole world seems to shake
I hear pitter-patter, pitter-patter on the window
That must be the rain
Then it stops, thank goodness!

Abi Lucia Brown (9)
Great Dalby Primary School, Melton Mowbray

Sea

Waves crashing against the rocks
Dolphins in the distance
Waves galloping like a herd of horses
Surfers in the white horse waves
Sunset over the sea like a red fireball
Sun rising like a yellow button
Seagulls awake and the sea is calm
The world is silent as the day begins
All I can smell is the salty sea.

Alex Murray (9)
Great Dalby Primary School, Melton Mowbray

Sister

My sister is like a storm
Every time she cuddles up to me she makes me warm

My sister is cuddly
My sister is cute
Just like a soft teddy bear
And every time I play with her it makes me happy.

Alex Kirk (8)
Great Dalby Primary School, Melton Mowbray

Sun

The sun is a bouncy ball rolling down the lane
A fireball, a petal, an autumn leaf
The sun is a bright light shimmering and glittering
A juicy orange, a smiley face, a swaying flower head.

Emma Sunderland (9)
Great Dalby Primary School, Melton Mowbray

Feelings

When I'm feeling bad I feel quite sad
When I'm feeling tough I feel quite rough
When I'm feeling down I go into a frown
When I feel low I don't know where to go.

Luke Johnson (9)
Great Dalby Primary School, Melton Mowbray

The Wolf

The wolf, grey and fast
It moves stealthily through the trees
It's big, vicious teeth and savage claws at the ready
It strikes and brings down its prey
It howls in the moonlight
And settles down to devour its food.

Thomas Kowalski (9)
Great Dalby Primary School, Melton Mowbray

Weather

The weather is furious
The weather is smooth
Summer is ending
Autumn is starting
Birds are leaving
The cold is coming.

Luke Harrison (10)
Great Dalby Primary School, Melton Mowbray

The Dragon's Dream

The dragon's dream on a sunny day
With lots of time to play,
Where everything's perfect,
And there's nothing to neglect.

Where there's a delicious feast,
And not a single beast,
Just a dragon's dream on a sunny day
Where the path of happiness leads the way.

Bethany Houghton (9)
Great Dalby Primary School, Melton Mowbray

Cheetah

The fast, furious predator
Races along the plains
No trees in its way,
So it has a good meal today.
The black and yellow body
It's the fastest in the world.

Niamh Gibson (10)
Great Dalby Primary School, Melton Mowbray

My Dream Of Seals

I've always dreamt to see a seal
To feel it and touch its silky skin
And his nose all rough and soggy
And to see him breathe out and in.

I've always dreamt to swim
With a seal to see all the beautiful creatures in the sea
Best of all to whiz past seaweed
The smell is so fresh and the clam-shells
Are in your hair.
You look like a mermaid.

Lydia Hall (9)
Great Dalby Primary School, Melton Mowbray

My Dreams

My dreams are absolutely crazy
Colours swirl round my mind
When I have scary dreams
I always have to find a key to unlock a tunnel
Where my buttons run
I see my brain pumping
And then the sun shines
A beam of light comes into my room
My alarm clock rings
I have to say that dreams are the weirdest thing.

Georgia Boorn (9)
Great Dalby Primary School, Melton Mowbray

Xmas

The wind blows,
The lakes flow
The leaves fall
The breeze is cool
The first flake is down
Autumn has ended
Two weeks till Xmas
What has Santa got?
Maybe a soldier for you
And a teddy or two
Xmas has gone
You've got your presents
The flakes are down
Nearly New Year
Snowmen have gone.

Harry Wells (10)
Great Dalby Primary School, Melton Mowbray

Breakfast In The Morning

I love the smell of bacon, eggs and beans
When I wake up in the morning
They make me feel warm and cosy inside
Sometimes I add fried bread and butter
It melts in my mouth and sometimes
The butter drips down my chin.

Dan Turner (8)
Great Dalby Primary School, Melton Mowbray

The Lonely Cat

There lying on my bed the lonely cat
All hot and bothered
When I go out somewhere I miss her
She's got no one to care for
Out of all my cats I love her best
She is so soft like a feather
She glares at me with her green eyes as if she likes me
Her ears are really clean and pink
I know she's waiting for me somewhere in the dark and gloomy night
I have no cat to play with
My cat can no longer sit on my lap
I really miss my cat when she has gone to rest
She chases around on my knee
My beautiful cat returned and free.

Sophie Lee (10)
Great Dalby Primary School, Melton Mowbray

My Cats

These cats like clawing my chairs
They like eating the meat on my plate like hungry foxes
They like sleeping on my bed all day long,
My cats like looking round the fence ready to pounce at the mice
and birds
They like sitting on my window sill watching the cars go by
The like climbing up trees and getting stuck
My cats like sitting in the sun washing themselves like they're
in the bath
My cats like fighting each other like wrestlers
My cats like making holes in my neighbour's garden like dogs
My cats are babies playing with wool and string
My cats like sleeping on my lap
My cats don't like water and they don't like getting wet
My cats don't like the cold
My cats don't like visiting the vet
They don't like the sound of the Hoover
They don't like the big booming bangs
My cats don't like being ignored
My cats don't like the rustling of silver foil
My cats can growl like a tiger
They can screech like a bird
They can hunt like a lion
My cats are woolly jumpers
My cats have huge eyes like two balls of fire
Swish! Goes my cats' tails swishing in the moonlight
My cats fall asleep
Zzzzzzzzzzzzzzzz!

Mollie Brooks (10)
Great Dalby Primary School, Melton Mowbray

The One, The Only Chocolate

Its creamy texture melts in your mouth
Like ice cream on a sunny day
We're not worthy of its velvety coating,
And still it hypnotizes us with its
Amazing, addictive taste.

Its decorated bars look as cool as a brand
New Ferrari driving by
Its silky brown colour looks so good that we dare look
It comes in all shapes and sizes like footballs or bunnies
There is only one more thing to say and
That is chocolate rules!

Harry Jinks (11)
Great Dalby Primary School, Melton Mowbray

The Match

Thousands of supporters watch in amazement,
The famous magicians start their magic.
All of a sudden the crowd roar like a nuclear bomb
Exploding when Steven Gerrard sends the ball into the net.
Gerrard skids across the grass.

Finally it quietens down,
Liverpool pass around
At full-time the whistle blows,
The crowd cheer as Liverpool celebrate.
The cup is theirs.

Matt Kuzmicz (10)
Great Dalby Primary School, Melton Mowbray

The Last Shot

The whistle blew
The whole world held their breath
Each step pounded in people's heads
The foot came in contact with the ball
There was an explosion that echoed for miles around
Sweat rolled down the side of his face and dripped to the ground
The ball spun uncontrollably like a black and white planet curling
round the pitch
The goalie leapt like a frog jumping to a lily pad
And he touched it.

The ball curled into the net
There was a sudden roar of cheers and the people laughed ecstatically
The tired players screamed with joy as they did a victory lap around
the pitch
The whistle blew
The end of the match
The deafening yeahs and nos were like a tiger's roar
The losers walked gloomily to their changing room
While the winners lead on their millions of fans, singing their anthem
A long time later they left the pitch and in the changing room they
cheered and screamed,
'Victory!'

Leah Topham (10)
Great Dalby Primary School, Melton Mowbray

My Secret Shipwreck Under The Sea!

I stepped onto the burning sand and stared
Sticking out of the waves, a large piece of wood?
I was curious, what was it?
I found myself moving slowly towards the shimmering sea.
Glittering under the sun
Before I knew it I had plunged into the depths of the tranquil,
                                        turquoise ocean.

As I hit the freezing ocean my foot hit a hard surface
Like a boot to a ball
A small wooden house?
A large stable?
No, it's a ship!
A shipwreck at the bottom of the sea!

I swam through a small porthole, a space between two worlds.
As I entered this enchanted world
I could smell the fresh smell of peppermint
I could hear the sweet sound of mermaids singing
It was bliss.

As I got further into this beautiful setting
I realised that I was not the only explorer
Lots of tiny colourful fishes swam at my side
They weaved in and out of the rocks and seaweed
Like a basketball player heading for the basket.

There was not a patch of dullness in my secret ship under the sea
All was colourful, all was bright
The not so beautiful and peaceful world was pulling me back up
                                        to its surface
Bye-bye my secret shipwreck under sea.

Rebecca Bond (10)
Great Dalby Primary School, Melton Mowbray

The Angry Troll

His eyes are like cats
As red as blood
His fur is as black as coal
His feet are gigantic elephant's feet
His claws are as sharp as needles.

He is small and stocky
But as strong as a bear
He will creep up behind you
And give you a scare

When he gets angry he stamps his feet
Shaking the ground like an earthquake
Get in his way and he will shriek
Roaring as loud as a furious lion.

Charlotte Brown (10)
Great Dalby Primary School, Melton Mowbray

The Game

The players come out looking as fresh as a spring morning
It's kick-off time and the players are ready to rumble
The whistle blows and it's all go
The fans are cheering as loud as a vicious lion roaring
A big free kick comes in the box and a player volleys
It in as fast as a cheetah.

A fantastic goal, we're in the lead
The players celebrate, will they keep it up?
Five minutes left and it's touch and go
The players are as tired as a professional runner running 20 miles.
It's the end of the game and the whistle blows
Everybody celebrates a happy end.

Toby Heaver (10)
Great Dalby Primary School, Melton Mowbray

Running

I tie up my shoelaces
I won't trip in the races
I try my best to run fast
So I don't come last.

The race may be short
The race may be long
If I lose I'll be distraught
If I win I'll sing a song.

There are three medals at the end
I'm in first as I round the bend
I am aiming to get gold
That's the one I want to hold.

It's a sprint down the straight
At this moment I feel great
The crowd are all cheering
The end is ever nearing.

There's nothing to choose between us all
We are all taking care not to fall
The pain and hurt is almost done
I've done it, at last I've *won!*

Lucy Sparling (10)
Great Dalby Primary School, Melton Mowbray

Goals, Goals, Goals

When you score a goal it feels good
But when you score an own goal it feels bad
When you save a goal you feel like you're on top of the world
But when you miss a penalty you hear boos all around you
And it echoes all around
When you score the winning penalty
You feel like you've win the lottery jackpot.

Edward Groom (10)
Great Dalby Primary School, Melton Mowbray

The Rose-Red Rose!

The rosy rose sits in an old dirty garden doing nothing!
It's twinkling petals glistening in the sun like gems
Thorns as sharp as swords waiting to strike
Leaves as green as bright sparkling emeralds
Sun beaming down on this one red rose
And thousands of weeds
Grass dead and brown
Sky as blue as sapphire
The rose sits silently in the garden!

Rosie Burrows (10)
Great Dalby Primary School, Melton Mowbray

Chocolate

The chocolaty taste of chocolate
Tastes like soup on a winter's day
The different colours and tastes melt in your mouth
Like ice cream on a summer's afternoon
The yummy taste of Galaxy, Mars, Lion, Crunchie,
Smoothly crushes in your mouth
Waiting, just waiting to run down our throats
As quickly as water going down a drain.

Hannah Burrows (10)
Great Dalby Primary School, Melton Mowbray

Lightning

High, high above the clouds is a castle where lady lightning lives
It is so beautiful
It has a golden door in the shape of lightning
Inside it's got guns and bombs that shoot lightning bolts
She makes a crackling voice

She can hear thunder coming and she gets so frustrated
And she goes into a strop like a three-year-old
She starts to throw bombs and shoots lightning bolts
And she lights up the night
Soon the thunder goes and she floats away peacefully.

Adam Wright (10)
Great Dalby Primary School, Melton Mowbray

My Imaginary Horse

My imaginary horse has a sparkling white-coloured coat
Piercing eyes are glistening emeralds staring up at the Earth's moon
Magical wings are opening flowers already waking to God's
                                        morning raindrops
His long swishy tail is like the ocean's waves crashing into the rocks
His horn is like a twirling slide looking into the future
A beautiful mane is a long spinning roundabout touching his knee
As I climb onto his back and fly upon the moonlit sky.

Hetty Burke (10)
Great Dalby Primary School, Melton Mowbray

The Circus

The spotlight is on us
And we're waiting to shine
Like a star in the night
All twinkling and bright
Sparkling glitter
Is like tinsel hanging on a decorated Christmas tree
All the crowds give applause
As they watch us all in awe
Spinning plates spin as fast as racing car wheels
Some of them are hitting the ground
Then carry on spinning around
The clowns they are funny
They make you laugh
They make you cry
Just watch out or they might hit you with a pie
Watch out for them as they pass by
Juggling balls
Up in the air
They look amazing
They make you stare
With a crash and a clang and a whole shebang goes by
We all sang
Come join the circus
You will have so much fun
And it's only just begun.

Georgina Kilpatrick (10)
Great Dalby Primary School, Melton Mowbray

The Sun!

I wake up in the morning
For only one thing
To see the sunrise
In all her glory
She glitters like a diamond
Shining out all over the world
All through the day
Her smiling face
Keeps me as warm as toast.

Later when it's time for bed
She's a red ruby
Gradually she disappears
Turning the sky bright red
I'm really sad when she goes away
But I know in my heart
She'll return tomorrow
Blazing like a red-hot fire
Once more!

Megan Story (10)
Great Dalby Primary School, Melton Mowbray

School Leaves

Only school leaves
Twist and twirl
Only school leaves
Curl and swirl
Only school leaves
Bathe in the sun
Only school leaves
Run and run.

Selina Jones (9)
Highley Primary School, Highley

How To Tame A Dragon

First, take some ancient gloop, magical and green
Next, the difficult bit, take an eyeball from a lion, tall and lean
Third, a particle of dust buried between two old pizzas
(Your brother's room is a good place to look).
Fourth, take some salamander's blood eaten by your teachers
Mix it up in a pot of grey clouds
Saying the magic words, 'Sistra, threymore, kumos, erachsi.'
Throw in a black widow and it's done
Find a dragon's cave and draw a circle outside
When he comes out start the fun
Throw the potion onto him and say,
'Ishcare, somuk, eromyerht, artsis.'
He'll freeze but not for long.
Then pull out an ancient sword and bang it on an Egyptian gong
The dragon, in the circle will appear and unfreeze.
He'll be yours for seven moons, then you'll need some
                                    magic remedies.
Heed my warnings, all of you and let him go at six
When you immediately eat several water sticks
This is the end of my recipe,
Don't throw it away, keep it, you'll thank me one day.

Tim Resch (10)
Highley Primary School, Highley

My Cat

I have a weird cat,
He's blue and hairy,
If you ever see it
You would think he's scary.

In the night,
He walks down the lane,
Digs up the flowers,
Even leaves fur on the drain.

If you think that's weird,
He eats toast,
Beans and bacon,
He likes that the most.

Will Bloomer (10)
Highley Primary School, Highley

Rabbit Poem

There is a rabbit in my garden,
He comes every day.
I didn't notice him at lunchtime,
But then he ran away.
I was puzzled and felt stupid,
I didn't know what to do.
So I went back home to have
Pea and ham stew.

David Hartmann (9)
Highley Primary School, Highley

Bullying

Bullies!
Bullies, bullies aren't good.
They think they're smart
But they're not hard.
They hide around corners
And scare the little ones.
They hit and kick and ask for money.
Bullies, bullies are horrible
They walk 'cool' and wear hoodies.
Bullies, bullies aren't nice
They creep around children
Like they're trying to be nice
But bullies, bullies are *not* nice!

Rebecca Phillips (9)
Highley Primary School, Highley

Michael Owen

There was an old man called Owen
He broke his leg by taking a throw-in.
He woke up in hospital with nowt but a book,
Along came the England squad to wish him good luck.
He came on the pitch and took a free kick
Along came Lampard and hit him with a brick.
There he was in the same hospital bed
Without any crutches but a bandage round his head!

Joshua Ward (10)
Highley Primary School, Highley

My Dad

My dad loves cooking and wrestling
He watches it on TV
He likes spiking his hair up
He gets drunk on weekends
Sometimes on Fridays he likes buying CDs
He likes to play on his Xbox 360 every day
He likes going shopping for DVDs
He likes going on his laptop buying things off the Internet
He loves his money too.

Jack Broome (10)
Highley Primary School, Highley

My Weird Dog

I have a weird dog,
That can see through dirty fog.
He plays with his hard blue ball,
When it pours down with rain but he aint small
Then he comes in covered in mud
Like all silly dogs would
He likes to play tug-of-war
But his gums bleed and go all sore.

Ben Richards (10)
Highley Primary School, Highley

Animals

A pes, swinging on the treetops,
N ewts, sitting around waiting for bees,
I nsects, jumping around in the grass,
M ice, crawling through little holes,
A nteaters, eating ants and maggots,
L eopards, racing like lightning,
S nakes, slithering round and round

All the animals have gone to sleep,
Now there's a bit of peace to keep.

Danielle Walker (10)
Highley Primary School, Highley

My Grandad

Since the day my grandad went,
My nanny Bett has been so glum
Every night there is a tear
For each memory of my grandad dear.

My grandad was a lovely man,
Even though he argued with my nan.
He played football for Highley,
He scored lots of goals against other teams.

He liked to watch me play football,
Jumped up and down when we scored a goal.
I feel like there's a hole in my heart,
My grandad played a real part.

Gregory Stevens (9)
Highley Primary School, Highley

Alone Child

In the darkness of a misty lair
Lay a child cold and bare
Abandoned by her mom and dad
She lay there unhealthy and sad.

The little girl laid there crying every night
No bear to hug, not even a light
No mum who would tuck her up in bed
Not even a pillow to rest her sleepyhead.

The walls were wet in the abandoned house
All she had for a friend was a tiny mouse
The floor was damp and had loads of mould
The whole room was horrible and was very cold.

Let's just say her life was short
The house is still there by the old abandoned port.

Ellie Jones (9)
Highley Primary School, Highley

The Witches' Spell

(Based on Macbeth)

Double, double, toil and trouble,
Fire burn and cauldron bubble.
Fillet of a loathsome sage,
In the cauldron, left to age.
Eye of head that has no shoulders,
Two mossy skulls like grinning boulders.
Leg of ant, feeler of snail,
Head of kitten, young weasel's tail.
For a charm to release Kronos,
Lava spurts; a certain bonus.
Double, double, toil and trouble,
Fire burn and cauldron bubble.
Eye of cyclops, Chimera's horn,
Hydra's veins, ripped and torn.
Phoenix feather, unicorn's mane,
Let this spell create much pain.
Celtic skin complete with woad,
Poisoned sickness, we do bode.
Double, double, toil and trouble,
Fire burn and cauldron bubble.

Joseph Wilmore (10)
Lees Primary School, Keighley

The Witches' Spell

(Based on Macbeth)

'Double, double, toil and trouble
Fire burn and cauldron bubble'.
Fillet of poisoned human liver,
In the cauldron a leverett that quivers,
Featherless wing of owl and decayed tooth of rat,
Parrot's beak and red-eyed cat,
Grasshopper leg and millipede lung,
Bewildered, senseless otter and ladybird dung
For a charm of death and disease,
Make this broth that looks like ravished fleas.
'Double, double, toil and trouble
Fire burn and cauldron bubble'.
Veins of Hercules, arteries of Harpies;
Mixed with rotting Cyclops' knees,
Dead shark on the beach,
Half-eaten by the leech;
Intestine of baby worm,
Death by infectious germs.
'Double, double, toil and trouble
Fire burn and cauldron bubble'.

Jethro Rainford (10)
Lees Primary School, Keighley

The Witches' Spell

(Based on Macbeth)

'Double, double, toil and trouble
Fire burn and cauldron bubble'.
Fillet of a mysterious bull,
In the cauldron with a cracked toad skull;
Claw of lizard and finger of possessed chimp
All mixed up with lashings of raw shrimp.
Deafened cat and snail's slime,
Dog's tail and dried-up slug with no more time
For a charm of endless slaughter,
Like a sheep drowned in poisoned water.
'Double, double, toil and trouble
Fire burn and cauldron bubble'.
Nail from Harpies, fang of vampire,
Warlocks' skeletons, burning fire.
A sabre-toothed tiger in its den,
Branch of willow, fire-breathing dragon in its pen
Lips of snakes
Hags in to bake.
'Double, double, toil and trouble
Fire burn and cauldron bubble'.

Liam Walsh (10)
Lees Primary School, Keighley

The Witches' Spell

(Based on Macbeth)

'Double, double, toil and trouble
Fire burn and cauldron bubble'.
Fillet of an eagle's eye
In the cauldron a squashed butterfly
Heart of lion and tail of rat
Teeth of wolf and claws of cat.
Human's ear and fish's skin
Donkey's tail and turtle's fin.
For a charm of evil from Hell
Like a murderer released from his cell
'Double, double, toil and trouble
Fire burn and cauldron bubble'.
Minotaur's horn and spider's web
Vampire veins and monkey head
Feather of phoenix and horse's hair
Eye of camel and leg of bear
Nose of frog and a branch off a tree
Don't let anything go free
'Double, double, toil and trouble
Fire burn and cauldron bubble'.

Samuel Treece (10)
Lees Primary School, Keighley

The Witches' Spell

(Based on Macbeth)

'Double, double, toil and trouble
Fire burn and cauldron bubble'.
Fillet of a big fat goose
In the cauldron goes a moose
Eye of cow and toe of bat
Wool of tiger and tongue of rat
Liver of a howling wolf, a spike of a hedgehog's sting
Head of dog and a bee with one wing
For a charm to work on living things
Like a hound that never brings
'Double, double, toil and trouble
Fire burn and cauldron bubble'.
Hair of rabbit and a vein of a bear
Which is mine, care or hair
Of the ravinal wish shake
The water of a lake, that has been taken in the dim of day
Liver of a howling beast
A gull that has been strangled for a feast
'Double, double, toil and trouble
Fire burn and cauldron bubble'.

Charlotte Brown (10)
Lees Primary School, Keighley

The Witches' Spell

(Based on Macbeth)

'Double, double, toil and trouble
Fire burn and cauldron bubble'.
Fillet of a white goat's ear
In the cauldron brewed like beer.
Tongue of wolf, teeth of rats,
Parrot's beak and red-eyed cats.
Giants' knees, whales' eyes
Sting of a bee and children's pies.
For a charm to make one sick
Like a snake gooey and slick.
'Double, double, toil and trouble
Fire burn and cauldron bubble'.

Benjamin Dixon (10)
Lees Primary School, Keighley

The Witches' Spell

(Based on Macbeth)

'Double, double, toil and trouble
Fire burn and cauldron bubble'.
Fillet of French frog
In the cauldron rotting hairs of a dead dog
Tail of dog and ear of rat
Gnawed on by a deadly cat
Knobbly knees and blubber of whale
Throw in an old snail
For a charm of instant death
Like a spell that takes men's breath
'Double, double, toil and trouble
Fire burn and cauldron bubble'.
Paw of wolf and skull of boy
Throw in the cauldron like a toy
Shell of snail and skin of snake
In the pot left to bake
Feathers of owl and eye of shark
The dead dog begins to growl and bark
'Double, double, toil and trouble
Fire burn and cauldron bubble'.

Jack Kavanagh (10)
Lees Primary School, Keighley

The Witches' Spell

(Based on Macbeth)

'Double, double, toil and trouble
Fire burn and cauldron bubble'.
Fillet of a fat pig's ear
In the cauldron, pickled deer
Eye of cow and tail of dead rat
Tongue of puppy and wing of bat
Snail's shell and a three-legged cat's whiskers
A blind man's silent whisper
For a charm of evil sadness
Like a life-time of torturing badness
'Double, double, toil and trouble
Fire burn and cauldron bubble'.
Eyelash of chimp, fingernail of rat
Vein of cat and hair of bat
Spike of porcupine and a great big feast
Hoof of cow and lips of a beast
'Double, double, toil and trouble
Fire burn and cauldron bubble'.

Bethany Nixon (10)
Lees Primary School, Keighley

The Witches' Spell

(Based on Macbeth)

'Double, double, toil and trouble
Fire burn and cauldron bubble'.
Fillet of a frozen frog
In the cauldron like a wooden log
Eye of a goat, toe of an owl
Fur of a tiger that cannot growl
Dead horn and a warm bee's sting
Dragon's leg and a bat's wide wing
For a charm a poisonous spider's leg
Like an eagle's new slimy egg
'Double, double, toil and trouble
Fire burn and cauldron bubble'.
Scale of a fish, bone of a cat
Wizard's mummy and a tongue of a bat
'Double, double, toil and trouble
Fire burn and cauldron bubble'.

Hannah Inman (10)
Lees Primary School, Keighley

The Witches' Spell

(Based on Macbeth)

'Double, double, toil and trouble
Fire burn and cauldron bubble'.
Fillet of a soul of a sly shark
And make it come out at dark
Tail of a cat, wing of a bat
Claw of a vulture and eye of a rat
Dragon's fire, everyone's desire
Unfortunately he killed the space
For a charm to rescue the lunch
Feed them like they've never been fed
'Double, double, toil and trouble
Fire burn and cauldron bubble'.
Fillet of a poor tiger, fur from a werewolf
Throw it down with a great big gulp
Tooth of a sabre-toothed tiger, what a flavour
To kill your neighbour
Baboon's arm stuck in a barn
Where everyone keeps calm.

Connor Fox (10)
Lees Primary School, Keighley

The Witches' Spell

(Based on Macbeth)

Fillet of a stewed baboon
In the cauldron kaboom balloons
Tongue of an old buried ear of grey cat
Horse's tail hair and claw of a strangled bat
Evil laugh and eye of tiger
Slice of slug and widowed spider
For a charm of changing bodies
Add an evil devil
Horn of fairy, lash of bull
Teeth of Dracula, Cyclops' skull
Vein of fairy
Horse's hoof and all that dairy
Lord of Warlocks in the pot
Then you add a devil's spot
Pour and sip from this big apple
Drink it and use the spell.

Adele Cowan (10)
Lees Primary School, Keighley

The Witches' Spell

(Based on Macbeth)

'Double, double, toil and trouble
Fire burn and cauldron bubble'.
Fillet of a pink pig's tail
In the cauldron the pig so pale
Leg of spider and toenail of cat
Fur of a polar bear and a tongue of a bat
Tiger's feet and a warm bee's sting
Goat's leg and a wizard's ping
For a charm of lizard's leg
To a month-old egg
Scale of fish, bone of dog
Tiger's mummy, eyeball of frog
The nose of a pig and the brain of a bee
Root of a lion's tooth and a gruesome key
'Double, double, toil and trouble
Fire burn and cauldron bubble'.

Jodie Packer (10)
Lees Primary School, Keighley

The Witches' Spell

(Based on Macbeth)

'Double, double, toil and trouble
Fire burn and cauldron bubble'.
Fillet of a leopard's nose
In the cauldron left to rot is a rotten old eye
Of a soldier and a smelly old rat
With a flattened old bat
Claws of a tiger, lung of a frog
Wizard's tongue and with a barking young dog
'Double, double, toil and trouble
Fire burn and cauldron bubble'.

Natalie Stephens (10)
Lees Primary School, Keighley

The Witches' Spell

(Based on Macbeth)

'Double, double, toil and trouble
Fire burn and cauldron bubble'.
Fillet of frozen frog
In the cauldron thick as smog
Knuckle of bull, eye of bat and fur of cat
Spike of a hedgehog, tall as a slug
For a charm of good luck
Like a bell from a duck
'Double, double, toil and trouble
Fire burn and cauldron bubble'.
Skull of snake, burn of fish
Witches' pet now and wish
'Double, double, toil and trouble
Fire burn and cauldron bubble'.

Victoria Milner (10)
Lees Primary School, Keighley

The Witches' Spell

(Based on Macbeth)

'Double, double, toil and trouble
Fire burn and cauldron bubble'.
Fillet of a furry cat
In the cauldron left like a rat
Eye of frog and toe of bat
And with the fur of an ancient cat
Spider leg and toe of frog
Slimy snake and crab bake
For a charm of tiger's liver
Like a trunk of falcon's nipper
'Double, double, toil and trouble
Fire burn and cauldron bubble'.
Fur of wolf, tooth of bat
Crumpled bones crushed and flat
'Double, double, toil and trouble
Fire burn and cauldron bubble'.

Courtney Dunstan (10)
Lees Primary School, Keighley

The Witches' Spell

(Based on Macbeth)

'Double, double, toil and trouble
Fire burn and cauldron bubble'.
Fillet of frozen bat
In the cauldron with a cat
Eye of a dying human
Whose name is Mr Truman
Poisonous spiders crawling up and down
Angry sharks lurking with a frown
For a charm, a spider's leg
Like a flying bird's egg
Scale of snake, tooth of dog
Giant's baby with a frog
'Double, double, toil and trouble
Fire burn and cauldron bubble'.

Rebecca Williams (10)
Lees Primary School, Keighley

The Witches' Spell

(Based on Macbeth)

'Double, double, toil and trouble
Fire burn and cauldron bubble'.
Fillet of frozen calf,
Head in the cauldron left like dead.
Eye of a toad, claw of a tiger that roars like mad
Trail of a slug and a person's eye
Disgusting toad and mosquito flies
For a charm of rage and fear
'Double, double, toil and trouble
Fire burn and cauldron bubble'.
Tusk of a rhino, feet of a dinosaur
'Double, double, toil and trouble
Fire burn and cauldron bubble'.

Alex Simkins (10)
Lees Primary School, Keighley

The Witches' Spell

(Based on Macbeth)

'Double, double, toil and trouble
Fire burn and cauldron bubble'.
Fillet of geese blood
In the cauldron soaked in mud
Eye of toad and toe of dog
Wool of goat and tongue of hog
Dragon's nose and bull horns
Chicken legs and a sting of a frog
For a charm of baby's blood
Like a mummy covered in mud
'Double, double, toil and trouble
Fire burn and cauldron bubble'.
Teeth of cheetah, beak of duck
With a spice of a stork
'Double, double, toil and trouble
Fire burn and cauldron bubble'.

Rhys Hart (10)
Lees Primary School, Keighley

The Witches' Spell

(Based on Macbeth)

'Double, double, toil and trouble
Fire burn and cauldron bubble'.
Fillet of a fried cat
In the cauldron a hairy bat
Claw of juicy rat and bony leg of dog
Wing of broken robin, mouldy log
Crab eye and French tiger's ear
Snake tongue and spider fear
For a charm, a breath of fire
Like a sign of no desire
'Double, double, toil and trouble
Fire burn and cauldron bubble'.
Eyebrows of Cyclops and horn of goat
Scale of snake, stinky ear that floats
'Double, double, toil and trouble
Fire burn and cauldron bubble'.

Taylor Robinson (11)
Lees Primary School, Keighley

The Witches' Spell

(Based on Macbeth)

'Double, double, toil and trouble
Fire burn and cauldron bubble'.
Fillet of grilled horse lung
In the cauldron with its tongue
Claws of strangled cat and eye of sleeping dog
Tail of monkey and scale of bleeding frog
Squid tentacles and lion's fur
Bat's wing and lizard's skin
For calm and powerful cream
Like a whirlwind of thoughtless dreams
'Double, double, toil and trouble
Fire burn and cauldron bubble'.
Feather of a Harpy's wing and veins of fairy
Touch of elephant and bulls that are wary
'Double, double, toil and trouble
Fire burn and cauldron bubble'.

Ellie Thornton (10)
Lees Primary School, Keighley

The Witches' Spell

(Based on Macbeth)

'Double, double, toil and trouble
Fire burn and cauldron bubble'.
Fillet of a newborn deer
In the cauldron for a year
Leg of rotting dog, claw of grilled rat
Arm of newt, wing of dead bat
Heart of baby baboon, a mouldy adult's thigh
Liver of a full grown monkey, a wasp's tiny eye
For a charm of rabbit's desire
Like a twister of reddening fire
'Double, double, toil and trouble
Fire burn and cauldron bubble'.
Scale of snake, horn of bull
Wings of fairy, human's skull
Shark's tooth, Minotaur's bellow
Image of buffalo, finger of a fine young fellow
'Double, double, toil and trouble
Fire burn and cauldron bubble'.

Lauren Pedley (10)
Lees Primary School, Keighley

The Witches' Spell

(Based on Macbeth)

'Double, double, toil and trouble
Fire burn and cauldron bubble'.
Fillet of an old aged deer
In the cauldron goes a pig's ear
Wing of bat, head of dog
Tail of cat, sleeping frog
Eyes of rat, leg of spider
Heart of snake, eye of tiger
For a charm of worthless bubble
Like a whirl of double trouble
'Double, double, toil and trouble
Fire burn and cauldron bubble'.
Tongue of badger, ear of hamster
Tooth of Minotaur, lungs of prankster
Veins of skunk, heart of monk
Organs of lion, a person called Bryan
'Double, double, toil and trouble
Fire burn and cauldron bubble'.

Adrian Wilson (10)
Lees Primary School, Keighley

Happiness

Happiness is bright yellow
It tastes like an ice lolly touching the tip of your tongue
It looks like an island with never-ending sand going through your toes
It smells like a roast turkey cooking in the oven
And sounds of fun and children laughing
It feels like warm air blowing in your face and your hair
                              is blowing about.

Emily Smout (9)
Northfield Road Primary School, Dudley

Happiness

Happiness is gold
It tastes like a nice chocolate cake melting in your mouth
It smells like flowers
It looks like a pot of gold at the end of a rainbow
It sounds like somebody cheering because they've won the jackpot
It feels like the warm sun shining down on you.

Darrin Tucker (9)
Northfield Road Primary School, Dudley

Happiness

Happiness is yellow like the bright sun
It tastes like a sweet stick of rock
Happiness smells like a fresh Monday morning
It looks like an enormous field with a thousand buttercups
Happiness sounds like the ocean swaying side to side
It feels like a soft, blue, comfy cushion.

Bethany Sidaway (9)
Northfield Road Primary School, Dudley

Loneliness

Loneliness is grey
It tastes like rotten eggs
It smells like dust
It looks like a poor animal being hurt
It sounds like a plank of wood
It feels like a cloud
Loneliness makes you unhappy
And it's hard to get out of
Loneliness is a nasty feeling, you get moody
Nobody wants to be lonely.

Karine Gilbert (9)
Northfield Road Primary School, Dudley

Happiness

Happiness is yellow
It tastes like melting chocolate and smells like fresh air
Happiness looks like the clouds floating in the sky
And sounds like the trees blowing in the wind
Happiness is a soft cuddly quilt wrapped warmly around you
Happiness is how everyone should feel!

Amber-Leigh Evans (10)
Northfield Road Primary School, Dudley

Love Is . . .

Love is a feeling which people share
Love is a feeling you can feel it spread
Love is a feeling
Love is first sight
Love is a thing
It's so bright.

Love can be high
Love can be low
Love is sometimes very slow
There's different kinds of love
Not just one
There's tons.

Tina Sultana (9)
Northfield Road Primary School, Dudley

What Is Love?

Love is the colour of the sky just before the sun sets
It tastes like a freshly cooked Sunday roast
And sounds like a piano playing a sweet love song
Love looks like a dreamy cloud
It smells like roses that have just bloomed
And it feels like a soft feather brushing across my face.

Alice Cox (9)
Northfield Road Primary School, Dudley

Happiness

Happiness is like the light blue sky
It tastes of delicious apple pie
And smells of flowers in your garden
It looks like waves crashing onto the shore
And sounds of birds singing their tune
Happiness feels like the summer in June.

Hajra Begum (9)
Northfield Road Primary School, Dudley

Happiness

Happiness is the colour of the blue morning sky
It tastes like the chocolate gateau in the fridge
It smells like the roses in the meadow
Happiness looks like the skipping lambs in the field
It sounds like the birds singing in the sky
It feels like someone surrounding me with love
Happiness is the best.

Elizabeth Willetts (9)
Northfield Road Primary School, Dudley

Happiness

Happiness is golden
It tastes like sugary sweets
Happiness smells like roses
It looks like a nice salad upon your plate
Happiness sounds like birds singing in a tree
It feels like a nice, warm, comfy bed.

Bethany Wood (9)
Northfield Road Primary School, Dudley

It Is Nice To Feel Happy

Happiness is bright yellow
It tastes like custard and chocolate cake
It smells like a summer rose
It looks like the golden sun
It sounds like the ripples of the sea
It feels like the warm summer sun.

Kerry Burgoyne (9)
Northfield Road Primary School, Dudley

Love

Love is red
It tastes like chocolate punch
It smells like dazzling roses
Love looks like a garden full of beautiful flowers
It sounds like birds singing
Love feels like something special that you can't let go!

Abidah Sultana (9)
Northfield Road Primary School, Dudley

Summer

S ummer is good
U nder the sun we play
M e and my friends
M y friends hide and I count
E very day we play the same game
R epeatedly.

Mathew Rogers (9)
Northfield Road Primary School, Dudley

Christmas

C hristmas lights everywhere
H aving a lot of fun
R elaxed on Christmas Day
I love Christmas
S uch fun
T winkling lights on the Christmas tree
M assive parcels for me
A ll around
S now is sparkling in front of my eyes.

Keiran Parkes (9)
Northfield Road Primary School, Dudley

My Trampoline - Haiku

It is brilliant
I jump and jump up and down
With my small sister.

Nicola Handley (9)
Northfield Road Primary School, Dudley

Books - Haiku

I like to read books
They are really good to read
I like them so much.

Amina Bibi (9)
Northfield Road Primary School, Dudley

Winter - Cinquain

Winter
Is very cold
It tips it down with snow
Everybody loves the winter
It's cold.

Natasha Bird (9)
Northfield Road Primary School, Dudley

Who Am I? - Haiku

I have long whiskers
I run quickly in long grass
Tell me who I am.

Ellie Cove **(9)**
Northfield Road Primary School, Dudley

Autumn - Haiku

Heat gone - back to school
The trees are bare, autumn's here
Winter's coming, yeah!

Bibi Muriyam (9)
Northfield Road Primary School, Dudley

Spring

S pring is coming, let's all go and play
P edalling down to the park
R acing with my dad
I win the race
N umber two for Dad today
G oing back home.

Sulaiman Janjua (9)
Northfield Road Primary School, Dudley

Summer

S wimming in the swimming pool
U sing all my energy
M ore people come in
M onkeying around
E njoying ourselves
R eady for dinner we all rush in.

James Whittingham (9)
Northfield Road Primary School, Dudley

What If?

What if I wake up late on Sunday?
What if I miss my match?
What if I miss three open goals?
What if we lose our match?
What if I forget to brush my teeth?
What if they all fall out?
What if I forget my homework?
What if the teacher gets cross?
What if I don't eat my meals?
What if I can't have treats?
What if my wheels fall off my bike?
What if I eat something I don't like?
What if I lose my books?
What if people give me funny looks?
What if I can't sing a note?
What if I lose my winter coat?
What if I get sick at night?
What if I wake up with a fright?
What if I don't be good?
What if I get covered in mud?

Liam Whitcombe (9)
Northfield Road Primary School, Dudley

What If?

What if the sun never came out?
What if all my mom did was shout?
What if my pet fish dies?
What if McDonald's stopped selling fries?
What if my dad never gave me money?
What if he only let me eat honey?
What if Jesus never rose from the dead?
What if I always had to make my bed?
What if my brother was nice to me?
What if my sister cooked the tea?
What if my dog was really a mouse?
What if my teacher lived in my house?

Caleb Burchell (9)
Northfield Road Primary School, Dudley

Freaky Life

What if I were six foot tall?
What if I would always fall?
What if I fell off a log?
What if I fell on a dog?
What if I saw a bat?
What if a bat freaked out a cat?
What if lightning strikes me?
Then my freaky life is beyond me!

Bradley Hanson (9)
Northfield Road Primary School, Dudley

What If?

What if I could fly?
What if I could touch the sky?
What if I didn't cry?
What if people didn't lie?
What if I didn't have school?
What if people weren't so cruel?
What if I could do magic?
What if I didn't have to eat cabbage?
What if I never got bored?
What if I became a lord?
What if I had a giant sword?
What if I never felt pain?
What if I became insane?

Christopher Hodgetts (9)
Northfield Road Primary School, Dudley

What If?

What if I had eight fingers on each hand?
What if I didn't come from this land?
What if the snow was black instead of white?
What if I had no left hand, but only a right?
What if my head was on my back?
What if my name was not Liam and I was known as Jack?

Liam Haycock (9)
Northfield Road Primary School, Dudley

The Little Blue Alien

On a planet
A blue alien
Was looking for a place to live
He looked over the planet
He wanted to look for a
Deep, dark, damp hole
Till he spotted it
The blue alien
Got some wood, bricks, cement
He went in the
Hole and
Started building himself a home.

Adam Dalton (8)
Offmore First School, Kidderminster

Do Aliens Exist?

Argh alien - never been seen before!
Swooping
Quickly around our planet
He crashed suddenly
There was
Red
Orange
Flames burning brightly
He jumped out of his ship
Fell into a tree
Nobody saw him.

Owen Scott (8)
Offmore First School, Kidderminster

Mysterious Space

Round and large planets
Aliens are suddenly sucked into the black hole
Deep
Dark

Comets and asteroids, burning like the sun
Space is
Quiet
Empty
Black

Stars glow and twinkle quietly
Spacemen are jumping on the moon
Slowly
Gently
Gracefully.

Kate Coomby (8)
Offmore First School, Kidderminster

Magical Space

Chocolate-swirled planet
A pitch-black world
Magical aliens singing joyfully
'A hot sizzling shooting star'
Shooting star, fragile dents
Little ball, round Earth,
Dusty like charcoal, floating through space
Little blobs of green, stupid and splodgy,
Bouncing up and down
Space is misty and magical
There's nothing more magical than space.

Hannah Watson (9)
Offmore First School, Kidderminster

Darkness

I think it's really lonely in space
It's so cold,
Cold
Enough to get frostbite
When I look far out
I can see dazzling
Glitter
Stars
I must admit
Space is *way* too big for a bedroom
I think it's real
Dull and rocky
Plus I'm conscious
That the sun might explode!
Even though
I'm 100 light years away.

Finola Carty (8)
Offmore First School, Kidderminster

Space Adventure

In dark space
It's empty
The only company
A few rocky planets
Cruising through in my spaceship
Looking through the portal
It's very dark up here
The only light
Stars
A meteor I just passed
Are my parents watching me on TV right now?

Matthew Knight (8)
Offmore First School, Kidderminster

Space Rhyme

It's dark in space
I quite like the dark
So I quite like space
You can see shooting stars
Everywhere
There's little shiny
Glittery
Dots on the planets
We're going to have a party
When I get back
It's cold
I go past the sun
It is shiny.

Olivia Humble (8)
Offmore First School, Kidderminster

I Miss Planet Earth

I don't like the dark
I can hear the rocket engines
Zooming
I can see the sun
Glowing bright
By the moon
It is very dusty
Rocky
On
The moon
It's very dark
I miss my mom and dad
I miss
Planet Earth.

Thomas Connor (8)
Offmore First School, Kidderminster